CONTINUO

50 Sonnets fror
The School of E

‘In 1799 special … introduced “utterly suppressing and prohibiting’’ by name the London Corresponding Society and the United Englishmen. Even the indefatigible conspirator, John Binns, felt that further national organisation was hopeless . . . When arrested he was found in possession of a ticket which was perhaps one of the last ‘‘covers’’ for the old L.C.S.:

Admit for the Season to the School of Eloquence.’

E. P. THOMPSON, *The Making of the English Working Class*

Works by Tony Harrison

POETRY

Earthworks
Newcastle is Peru
The Loiners
Palladas: Poems
from *The School of Eloquence* & other poems

THEATRE

Aikin Mata (with James Simmons)
The Misanthrope
Phaedra Britannica
Bow Down
The Passion
The Bartered Bride
The Oresteia

CONTINUOUS

50 Sonnets from

The School of Eloquence

TONY HARRISON

REX COLLINGS LONDON 1981

Heredity

How you became a poet's a mystery!
Wherever did you get your talent from?
I say: *I had two uncles, Joe and Harry—*
one was a stammerer, the other dumb.

Nunc mea Pierios cupiam per pectora fontes
Irriguas torquere vias, totumque per ora
Volvere laxatum gemino de vertice rivum;
Ut, tenues oblita sonos, audacibus alis
Surgat in officium venerandi Musa parentis.
Hoc utcunque tibi gratum, pater optime, carmen
Exiguum meditatur opus, nec novimus ipsi
Aptius a nobis quae possint munera donis
Respondere tuis, quamvis nec maxima possint
Respondere tuis, nedum ut par gratia donis
Esse queat, vacuis quae redditur arida verbis . . .

Si modo perpetuos sperare audebitis annos,
Et domini superesse rogo, lucemque tueri,
Nec spisso rapient oblivia nigra sub Orco,
Forsitan has laudes, decantatumque parentis
Nomen, ad exemplum, servo servabitis aevo.

John Milton (1637)

Contents

for
mam
&
dad

in memoriam

F.H. 1906–1976
H.A.H. 1903–1980

ONE

On Not Being Milton

for Sergio Vieira & Armando Guebuza (Frelimo)

Read and committed to the flames, I call
these sixteen lines that go back to my roots
my *Cahier d'un retour au pays natal*,
my growing black enough to fit my boots.

The stutter of the scold out of the branks
of condescension, class and counter-class
thickens with glottals to a lumpen mass
of Ludding morphemes closing up their ranks.
Each swung cast-iron Enoch of Leeds stress
clangs a forged music on the frames of Art,
the looms of owned language smashed apart!

Three cheers for mute ingloriousness!

Articulation is the tongue-tied's fighting.
In the silence round all poetry we quote
Tidd the Cato Street conspirator who wrote:

Sir, I Ham a very Bad Hand at Righting.

note: An 'Enoch' is an iron sledge-hammer used by the Luddites to smash the frames which were also made by the same Enoch Taylor of Marsden. The cry was: Enoch made them, Enoch shall break them!

The Rhubarbarians

I

Those glottals glugged like poured pop, each
rebarbative syllable, rememberancer, raise
'mob' *rhubarb-rhubarb* to a tribune's speech
crossing the crackle as the hayricks blaze.

The gaffers' blackleg Boswells at their side.
Horsfall of Ottiwells, if the bugger could,
'd've liked to (exact words recorded) *ride*
up to my saddle-girths in Luddite blood.

What t'mob said to the cannons on the mills,
shouted to soldier, scab and sentinel
's silence, parries and hush on whistling hills,
shadows in moonlight playing knurr and spell.

It wasn't poetry though. Nay, wiseowl Leeds
pro lege et lege schools, nobody needs
your drills and chanting to parrot right
the *tusky-tusky* of the pikes that night.

II

(On translating Smetana's *Prodanā Nevěsta* for the Metropolitan Opera, New York.)

One afternoon the Band Conductor up on his stand
Somehow lost his baton it flew out of his hand
So I jumped in his place and conducted the band
With mi little stick of Blackpool Rock!
George Formby

Finale of ACT II. Though I resist
blurring the clarity of *hanba* (shame)
not wanting the least nuance to be missed
syllables run to rhubarb just the same . . .

Sorry, dad, you won't get that quatrain
(I'd like to be the poet my father reads!)
It's all from you once saying on the train
how most of England's rhubarb came from Leeds.

Crochets and quavers, rhubarb silhouettes,
dark-shy sea-horse heads through waves of dung!
Rhubarb arias, duets, quartets
soar to precision from our common tongue.

The uke in the attic manhole once was yours!

Watch me on the rostrum wave my arms—

mi little stick of Leeds grown *tusky* draws
galas of rhubarb from the MET-set palms.

note: tusky: the Leeds word for rhubarb

Study

Best clock. Best carpet. Best three chairs.

For deaths, for Christmases, a houseless aunt,
for those too old or sick to manage stairs.

I try to whistle in it but I can't.

Uncle Joe came here to die. His gaping jaws
once plugged in to the power of his stammer
patterned the stuck plosive without pause
like a d-d-damascener's hammer.

Mi aunty's baby still. The dumbstruck mother.
The mirror, tortoise-shell-like celluloid
held to it, passed from one hand to another.
No babble, blubber, breath. The glass won't cloud.

The best clock's only wound for layings out
so the stillness isn't tapped at by its ticks.
The settee's shapeless underneath its shroud.

My mind moves upon silence and *Aeneid* VI.

Me Tarzan

Outside the whistled gang-call, *Twelfth Street Rag*,
then a Tarzan yodel for the kid who's bored,
whose hand's on his liana . . . no, back
to Labienus and his flaming sword.

Of laikin', then to t'fish 'oil all the boys,
off tartin', off to t'flicks but on, on, on,
the foldaway card table, the green baize,
De Bello Gallico and lexicon.

It's only his jaw muscles that he's tensed
into an enraged *shit* that he can't go;
down with polysyllables, he's against
all pale-face Caesars, *for* Geronimo.

He shoves the frosted attic skylight, shouts:

Ah bloody can't ah've gorra Latin prose.

His bodiless head that's poking out 's
like patriarchal Cissy-bleeding-ro's.

Wordlists

'There was only one more thing which had to be done, a last message to leave behind on the last day of all: and so he gathered up his strength in the midst of a long stretch of silence and framed his lips to say to me quite clearly the one word Dictionary.*'*
The Life of Joseph Wright (1885–1930)

I

Good parrots got good marks. I even got
a 100 in Divinity (posh schools' R.I.),
learned new long words and (wrongly stressed) *harlŏt*
I asked the meaning of so studiously.

I asked mi mam. She said she didn't know.
The Classics/R.I. master hummed and hawed.
(If only he'd've said it was a pro!)
New words: 'venery', 'VD' and 'bawd'!

Sometime . . . er . . . there's summat in that drawer . . .

photograph foetuses, a pinman with no prick,
things I learned out laiking years before
they serialised 'Life' in the *Sunday Pic.*

Words and wordlessness. Between the two
the gauge went almost ga-ga. No R.I.,
no polysyllables could see me through,
come glossolalia, dulciloquy.

II

The *Funk & Wagnalls*? Does that still survive?
Uncle Harry most eloquent deaf-mute
jabbed at its lexis till it leaped to life
when there were Tory errors to confute.

A bible paper bomb that dictionary.
I learned to rifle through it at great speed.
He's dead. I've studied, got the OED
and other tongues I've slaved to speak or read:

L & S dead Latin, L & S dead Greek,
one the now dead lexicographer gave me,
Ivan Poldauf, his English-Czech *slovník*;
Harrap's French 2 vols, a Swahili,
Cabrera's Afro-Cuban *Anagó*,
Hausa, Yoruba, both R.C. Abraham's—

but not the tongue that once I used to know
but can't bone up on now, and that's mi mam's.

III

The treasure found here on this freezing shore,
with last war tanktraps, and oil-clagged birds,
the morning shivery, the seawinds raw,
is the memory of a man collecting words.

Crushed scallops, washed up hard hats, shit, what fitter
thesaurus trove of trashes could he wish,
our lexicographer and *Doctor Litter-*
arum netting a fine but unexpected fish?

His heart beat faster when a living mouth
(the jotting said a 'fishwife's') used the old
and, for him forgotten in his flit down South,
border word *yagach* to describe the cold.

Though society 's not like the OED
and the future's just as yagach as the day,
I celebrate beside the same bleak sea
James Murray, and a scholar's clarion call
that set those sharp speech combers on their way:

Fling our doors wide! all, all, not one, but all!

Classics Society

(Leeds Grammar School 1552 1952)

The grace of Tullies eloquence doth excell
any Englishmans tongue . . . my barbarous stile . . .

The tongue our leaders use to cast their spell
was once denounced as 'rude', 'gross', 'base' and 'vile'.

How fortunate we are who've come so far!

We boys can take old Hansards and translate
the British Empire into S.P.Q.R.
but nothing demotic or too up-to-date,
and *not* the English that I speak at home,
not Hansard standards, and if Antoninus
spoke like delinquent Latin back in Rome
he'd probably get gamma double minus.

And so the lad who gets the alphas works
the hardest in his class at his translation
and finds good Ciceronian for Burke's:

a dreadful schism in the British nation.

National Trust

Bottomless pits. There's one in Castleton,
and stout upholders of our law and order
one day thought its depth worth wagering on
and borrowed a convict hush-hush from his warder
and winched him down; and back, flayed, grey, mad, dumb.

Not even a good flogging made him holler!

O gentlemen, a better way to plumb
the depths of Britain's dangling a scholar,
say, here at the booming shaft at Towanroath,
now National Trust, a place where they got tin,
those gentlemen who silenced the men's oath
and killed the language that they swore it in.

The dumb go down in history and disappear
and not one gentleman 's been brought to book:

Mes den hep tavas a-gollas y dyr

(Cornish)—
'the tongueless man gets his land took.'

Them & [uz]

for Professors Richard Hoggart & Leon Cortez

I

αἰαῖ, ay, ay! . . . stutterer Demosthenes
gob full of pebbles outshouting seas—

4 words only of *mi 'art aches* and . . . "Mine's broken,
you barbarian, T.W.!" *He* was nicely spoken.
"Can't have our glorious heritage done to death!"

I played the Drunken Porter in *Macbeth.*

"Poetry's the speech of kings. You're one of those
Shakespeare gives the comic bits to: prose!
All poetry (even Cockney Keats?) you see
's been dubbed by [ʌs] into RP,
Received Pronunciation, please believe [ʌs]
your speech is in the hands of the Receivers."

"We say [ʌs] not [uz] T.W.!" That shut my trap.
I doffed my flat a's (as in 'flat cap')
my mouth all stuffed with glottals, great
lumps to hawk up and spit out . . . *E-nun-ci-ate*!

II

So right, yer buggers, then! We'll occupy
your lousy leasehold Poetry.

I chewed up Littererchewer and spat the bones
into the lap of dozing Daniel Jones,
dropped the initials I'd been harried as
and used my *name* and own voice: [uz] [uz] [uz],
ended sentences with by, with, from,
and spoke the language that I spoke at home.
R.I.P. RP, R.I.P. T.W.
I'm *Tony* Harrison no longer you!

You can tell the Receivers where to go
(and not aspirate it) once you know
Wordsworth's *matter/water* are full rhymes,
[uz] can be loving as well as funny.

My first mention in the *Times*
automatically made Tony Anthony!

Working

Among stooped getters, grimy, knacker-bare,
head down thrusting a 3 cwt corf
turned your crown bald, your golden hair
chafed fluffy first and then scuffed off,
chick's back, then eggshell, that sunless white.
You strike sparks and plenty but can't see.
You've been underneath too long to stand the light.
You're lost in this sonnet for the bourgeoisie.

Patience Kershaw, bald hurryer, fourteen,
this wordshift and inwit's a load of crap
for dumping on a slagheap, I mean
th'art nobbut summat as wants raking up.

I stare into the fire. Your skinned skull shines.
I close my eyes. That makes a dark like mines.

Wherever hardship held its tongue the job
's breaking the silence of the worked-out gob.

note: 'gob': an old Northern coal-mining word for the space left after the coal has been extracted. Also, of course, the mouth, and speech.

Cremation

So when she hears him clearing his throat
every few seconds she's aware what he's raking
's death off his mind; the next attack. The threat
of his dying has her own hands shaking.

The mangle brought it on. Taking it to bits.
She didn't need it now he'd done with pits.

A grip from behind that seems to mean *don't go*
tightens through bicep till the fingers touch.
His, his dad's and *his* dad's lifetime down below
crammed into one huge nightshift, and too much.

He keeps back death the way he keeps back phlegm
in company, curled on his tongue. Once left alone
with the last coal fire in the smokeless zone,
he hawks his cold gobful at the brightest flame,
too practised, too contemptuous to miss.

Behind the door she hears the hot coals hiss.

TWO

Book Ends

I

Baked the day she suddenly dropped dead
we chew it slowly that last apple pie.

Shocked into sleeplessness you're scared of bed.
We never could talk much, and now don't try.

You're like book ends, the pair of you, she'd say,
Hog that grate, say nothing, sit, sleep, stare . . .

The 'scholar' me, you, worn out on poor pay,
only our silence made us seem a pair.

Not as good for staring in, blue gas,
too regular each bud, each yellow spike.

A night you need my company to pass
and she not here to tell us we're alike!

Your life's all shattered into smithereens.

Back in our silences and sullen looks,
for all the Scotch we drink, what's still between 's
not the thirty or so years, but books, books, books.

II

The stone's too full. The wording must be terse.
There's scarcely room to carve the FLORENCE on it—

Come on, it's not as if we're wanting verse.
It's not as if we're wanting a whole sonnet!

After tumblers of neat *Johnny Walker*
(I think that both of us we're on our third)
you said you'd always been a clumsy talker
and couldn't find another, shorter word
for 'beloved' or for 'wife' in the inscription,
but not too clumsy that you can't still cut:

You're supposed to be the bright boy at description
and you can't tell them what the fuck to put!

I've got to find the right words on my own.

I've got the envelope that he'd been scrawling,
mis-spelt, mawkish, stylistically appalling
but I can't squeeze more love into their stone.

Next Door

I

Ethel Jowett died still hoping not to miss
next year's *Mikado* by the D'Oyly Carte.
For being her 'male escort' (9!) to this
she gave my library its auspicious start:

The Kipling Treasury. My name. The date:
Tony Harrison   1946
in dip-in-penmanship type copperplate
with proper emphasis on thins and thicks.

Mi mam was 'that surprised' how many came
to see the cortege off and doff their hats—
All the 'old lot' left gave her the same
busing back from 'Homes' and Old Folk's Flats.

Since mi mam dropped dead mi dad's took fright.

His dicky ticker beats its quick retreat:

It won't be long before Ah'm t'only white!

Or t'Town Hall's thick red line sweeps through t'whole street.

II

Their front garden (8 x 5) was one of those
the lazier could write off as 'la-di-dah'.
Her brother pipesmoked greenfly off each rose
in summer linen coat and Panama.

Hard-faced traders tore her rooms apart.
Litter and lavender in ransacked drawers,
the yearly programmes for the D'Oyly Carte.
'Three Little Maids' she'd marked with '4 encores!'

Encore! No more. A distant relative
roared up on a loud bike and poked around.
Mi mam cried when he'd gone, and spat out: *Spiv!*

I got Tennyson and Milton leather-bound.

The Sharpes came next. He beat her, blacked her eye.
Through walls I heard each blow, each *Cunt! Cunt! Cunt!*

The Jowetts' dahlias were left to die.

Now mi dad's the only one keeps up his front.

III

Also the only one who shifts his snow
and him long past his three score years and ten.

You *try* to understand: *Their sort don't know.*
They're from the sun. But wait till they're old men.

But if some from out that 'old lot' still survive
and, shopping for essentials, shuffle past,
they'll know by your three clear flags that you're alive
and, though you'll never speak, they're not the last.

Outside your clearing your goloshes slip.
The danger starts the moment you're next door—
the fall, the dreaded 'dislocated hip',
the body's final freeze-up with no thaw.

If you weren't scared you'd never use the phone!

The winter's got all England in its vice.

All night I hear a spade that scrapes on stone
and see our street one skidding slide of ice.

IV

All turbans round here now, forget flat caps!

*They've taken over everything bar t'*CO-OP.
Pork's gone west, chitt'lins, trotters, dripping baps!
And booze an' all, if it's a Moslem owns t'new shop.

*Ay, t'*Off Licence, *that's gone Paki in t'same way!*
(You took your jug and bought your bitter draught)
Ah can't get over it, mi dad'll say,
smelling curry in a pop shop. Seems all daft.

Next door but one this side 's front room wi t'
Singers *hell for leather all day long 's*
some sort o' sweatshop bi the looks on it
running up them dresses . . . them . . . sarongs!

Last of the 'old lot' still left in your block.
Those times, they're gone. The 'old lot' can't come back.

Both doors I notice now you double lock—

he's already in your shoes, your next-door black.

Long Distance

I

Your bed's got two wrong sides. Your life's all grouse.
I let your phone-call take its dismal course:

Ah can't stand it no more, this empty house!

Carrots choke us wi'out your mam's white sauce!

Them sweets you brought me, you can have 'em back.
Ah'm diabetic now. Got all the facts.
(The diabetes comes hard on the track
of two coronaries and cataracts.)

Ah've allus liked things sweet! But now ah push
food down mi throat! Ah'd sooner do wi'out.
And t'only reason now for beer 's to flush
(so t'dietician said) mi kidneys out.

When I come round, they'll be laid out, the sweets,
Lifesavers, my father's New World treats,
still in the big brown bag, and only bought
rushing through JFK as a last thought.

II

Though my mother was already two years dead
Dad kept her slippers warming by the gas,
put hot water bottles her side of the bed
and still went to renew her transport pass.

You couldn't just drop in. You had to phone.
He'd put you off an hour to give him time
to clear away her things and look alone
as though his still raw love were such a crime.

He couldn't risk my blight of disbelief
though sure that very soon he'd hear her key
scrape in the rusted lock and end his grief.
He *knew* she'd just popped out to get the tea.

I believe life ends with death, and that is all.
You haven't both gone shopping; just the same,
in my new black leather phone book there's your name
and the disconnected number I still call.

Continuous

James Cagney was the one up both our streets.
His was the only art we ever shared.
A gangster film and choc ice were the treats
that showed about as much love as he dared.

He'd be my own age now in '49!
The hand that glinted with the ring he wore,
his father's, tipped the cold bar into mine
just as the organist dropped through the floor.

He's on the platform lowered out of sight
to organ music, this time on looped tape,
into a furnace with a blinding light
where only his father's ring will keep its shape.

I wear it now to Cagneys on my own
and sense my father's hands cupped round my treat—

they feel as though they've been chilled to the bone
from holding my ice cream all through *White Heat*.

Clearing

I

The ambulance, the hearse, the auctioneers
clear all the life of that loved house away.
The hard-earned treasures of some 50 years
sized up as junk, and shifted in a day.

A stammerer died here and I believe
this front room with such ghosts taught me my trade.
Now strangers chip the paintwork as they heave
the spotless piano that was never played.
The fingerprints they leave mam won't wipe clean
nor politely ask them first to wipe their boots,
nor coax her trampled soil patch back to green
after they've trodden down the pale spring shoots.

I'd hope my mother's spirit wouldn't chase
her scattered household, even if it could.
How could she bear it when she saw no face
stare back at her from that long polished wood?

II

The landlord's glad to sell. The neighbourhood,
he fears, being mostly black, 's now on the skids.
The gate my father made from bread-tray wood
groans at the high jinks of Jamaican kids.

Bless this house's new black owners, and don't curse
that reggae booms through rooms where you made hush
for me to study in (though I wrote verse!)
and wouldn't let my sister use the flush!

The hearse called at the front, the formal side.
Strangers used it, doctors, and the post.
It had a show of flowers till you died.
You'll have to use the front if you're a ghost,
though it's as flat and bare as the back yard,
a beaten hard square patch of sour soil.

Hush!
        Haunt me, and not the house!
                                        I've got to lard
my ghosts' loud bootsoles with fresh midnight oil:

Illuminations

I

The two machines on Blackpool's Central Pier,
The Long Drop and *The Haunted House* gave me
my thrills the holiday that post-war year
but my father watched me spend impatiently:

Another tanner's worth, but then no more!

But I sneaked back the moment that you napped.
50 weeks of ovens, and 6 years of war
made you want sleep and ozone, and you snapped:

Bugger the machines! Breathe God's fresh air!

I sulked all week, and wouldn't hold your hand.
I'd never heard you mention God, or swear,
and it took me until now to understand.

I see now all the piled old pence turned green,
enough to hang the murderer all year
and stare at millions of ghosts in the machine—

The penny dropped in time! Wish you were here!

II

We built and bombed Boche stalags on the sands,
or hunted for beached starfish on the rocks
and some days ended up all holding hands
gripping the pier machine that gave you shocks.
The current would connect. We'd feel the buzz
ravel our loosening ties to one tense grip,
the family circle, one continuous US!
That was the first year on my scholarship
and I'd be the one who'd make that circuit short.
I lectured them on neutrons and Ohm's Law
and other half-baked Physics I'd been taught.
I'm sure my father felt I was a bore!

Two dead, but current still flows through us three
though the circle takes for ever to complete—
eternity, annihilation, me,
that small bright charge of life where they both meet.

III

The family didn't always feel together.
Those silent teas with all of us apart
when no-one spoke except about the weather
and not about his football or my art.

And in those silences the grating sound
of father's celery, the clock's loud tick,
the mine subsidence from deep underground,
mi mam's loose bottom teeth's relentless click.

And when, I'm told, St. James's came to fetch her,
My teeth! were the final words my mother said.
Being without them, even on a stretcher,
was more undignified than being dead.

Ay! I might have said, *and put her in her box*
dressed in that long gown she bought to wear,
not to be outclassed by those posh frocks,
at her son's next New York première!

Turns

I thought it made me look more 'working class'
(as if a bit of chequered cloth could bridge that gap!)
I did a turn in it before the glass.
My mother said: *It suits you, your dad's cap.*
(She preferred me to wear suits and part my hair:
You're every bit as good as that lot are!)

All the pension queue came out to stare.
Dad was sprawled beside the postbox (still VR),
his cap turned inside up beside his head,
smudged H A H in purple Indian ink
and Brylcreem slicks displayed so folk might think
he wanted charity for dropping dead.

He never begged. For nowt! Death's reticence
crowns his life's, and *me*, I'm opening my trap
to busk the class that broke him for the pence
that splash like brackish tears into our cap.

Punchline

No! Revolution never crossed your mind!
For the kids who never made it through the schools
the Northern working class escaped the grind
as boxers or comedians, or won the pools.

Not lucky, no physique, too shy to joke,
you scraped together almost 3 weeks' pay
to buy a cast-off uke that left you broke.
You mastered only two chords, G and A!

That's why when I've heard George Formby that I've wept.
I'd always wondered what that thing was for,
I now know was a plectrum, that you'd kept,
but kept hidden, in your secret condom drawer.

The day of your cremation which I missed
I saw an old man strum a uke he'll never play,
cap spattered with tossed dimes. I made a fist
round my small change, your son, and looked away.

Marked With D.

When the chilled dough of his flesh went in an oven
not unlike those he fuelled all his life,
I thought of his cataracts ablaze with Heaven
and radiant with the sight of his dead wife,
light streaming from his mouth to shape her name,
'not Florence and not Flo but always Florrie'.
I thought how his cold tongue burst into flame
but only literally, which makes me sorry,
sorry for his sake there's no Heaven to reach.
I get it all from Earth my daily bread
but he hungered for release from mortal speech
that kept him down, the tongue that weighed like lead.

The baker's man that no-one will see rise
and England made to feel like some dull oaf
is smoke, enough to sting one person's eyes
and ash (not unlike flour) for one small loaf.

A Close One

Hawsers. Dirigibles. Searchlight. *Messerschmitts*.
Half let go. Half rake dark nowt to find . . .

Day old bereavement debris of a blitz
there's been no shelter from, no *all clear* whined.

Our cellar 'refuge room' made anti-gas.
Damp that smelled of graves not Morecambe Bay.
Air Raid Precautions out of *Kensitas*.
A Victory jig-saw on Fry's Cocoa tray.
Sandwiches. Snakes & Ladders. Thermos flask.

Sirens, then silences, then bombers' drone.
Long whistles. Windows gone. Each time I'd ask
which one was the Jerry, which our own.

How close we were with death's wings overhead!

How close we were not several hours ago.

These lines to hold the still too living dead—

my Redhill container, my long-handled hoe.

Blocks

A droning vicar bores the congregation
and misquotes *Ecclesiastes* Chapter 3.
If anyone should deliver an oration
it should be me, her son, in poetry.

All the family round me start to sob.
For all my years of Latin and of Greek
they'd never seen the point of 'for a job',
I'm not prepared to stand up now and speak.

A time to . . . plough back into the soil
the simple rhymes that started at her knee,
the poetry, that 'sedentary toil'
that began, when her lap was warm, with ABC.

Blocks with letters. Lettered block of stone.
I have to move the blocks to say farewell.

I hear the family cry, the vicar drone
and VALE, MATER 's all that I can spell.

Bringing Up

It was a library copy otherwise
you'd've flung it in the fire in disgust.
Even cremation can't have dried the eyes
that wept for weeks about my 'sordid lust.'

The undertaker would have thought me odd
or I'd've put my book in your stiff hand.
You'd've been embarassed though to meet your God
clutching those poems of mine that you'd like banned.

I thought you could hold my *Loiners*, and both burn!

And there together in the well wrought urn,
what's left of you, the poems of your child,
devoured by one flame, unreconciled,
like soots on washing, black on bone-ash white.

Maybe you see them in a better light!

But I still see you weeping, your hurt looks:

You weren't brought up to write such mucky books!

Timer

Gold survives the fire that's hot enough
to make you ashes in a standard urn.
An envelope of coarse official buff
contains your wedding ring which wouldn't burn.

Dad told me I'd to tell them at St. James's
that the ring should go in the incinerator.
That 'eternity' inscribed with both their names is
his surety that they'd be together, 'later'.

I signed for the parcelled clothing as the son,
this cardy, apron, pants, bra, dress—

the clerk phoned down: *6-8-8-3-1?*
Has she still her ring on? (Slight pause) *Yes*!

It's on my warm palm now, your burnished ring!

I feel your ashes, head, arms, breasts, womb, legs,
sift through its circle slowly, like that thing
you used to let me watch to time the eggs.

Fire-eater

My father speaking was like conjurors I'd seen
pulling bright silk hankies, scarves, a flag
up out of their inwards, red, blue, green,
so many colours it would make me gag.

Dad's eldest brother had a shocking stammer.
Dad punctuated sentence ends with but . . .
Coarser stuff than silk they hauled up grammar
knotted together deep down in their gut.

Theirs are the acts I nerve myself to follow.
I'm the clown sent in to clear the ring.
Theirs are the tongues of fire I'm forced to swallow
then bring back knotted, one continuous string
igniting long-pent silences, and going back
to Adam fumbling with Creation's names,
and though my vocal chords get scorched and black
there'll be a constant singing from the flames.

Background Material

My writing desk. Two photos, mam and dad.
A birthday, him. Their ruby wedding, her.
Neither one a couple and both bad.
I make out what's behind them from the blur.

Dad's in our favourite pub, now gone for good.
My father and his background are both gone,
but hers has my Welsh cottage and a wood
that still shows those same greens eight summers on,
though only the greenness of it 's stayed the same.

Though one of them 's in colour and one 's not,
the two are joined, apart from their shared frame,
by what, for photographers, would mar each shot:

in his, if you look close, the gleam, the light,
me in his blind right eye, but minute size—

in hers, as though just cast from where I write,
a shadow holding something to its eyes.

THREE

Self Justification

Me a poet! My daughter with maimed limb
became a more than tolerable sprinter.
And Uncle Joe. Impediment spurred him,
the worst stammerer I've known, to be a printer.

He handset type much faster than he spoke.
Those cruel consonants, *m*s, *p*s, and *b*s
on which his jaws and spirit almost broke
flicked into order with sadistic ease.

It seems right that Uncle Joe, 'b-buckshee
from the works', supplied those scribble pads
on which I stammered my first poetry
that made me seem a cissy to the lads.

Their aggro towards me, my need of them 's
what keeps my would-be mobile tongue still tied—

aggression, struggle, loss, blank printer's ems
by which all   eloquence   gets justified.

Divisions

I

All aggro in tight clothes and skinhead crops
they think that like themselves I'm on the dole.
Once in the baths that mask of 'manhood' drops.
Their decorated skins lay bare a soul.

Teenage dole-wallah piss-up, then tattoos.
Brown Ale and boys' bravado numbs their fright—
MOTHER in ivy, blood reds and true blues
against that North East skin so sunless white.

When next he sees United lose a match,
his bovvers on, his scarf tied round his wrist,
his rash NEWCASTLE RULES will start to scratch,
he'll aerosol the walls, then go get pissed . . .

So I hope the TRUE LOVE on your arm stays true,
the MOTHER on your chest stays loved, not hated.

But most I hope for jobs for all of you—

next year your tattooed team gets relegated!

II

Wartime bunkers, runways overgrown,
streets named for the town's two England caps;
cricket played with shovelblade and stone,
the daylight's rotten props near to collapse.

HEALTH (H changed to W) FOR ALL
with its *Never Have Another Haemorrhoid*
is all that decorates the tap-room wall
of this pub for pensioners and unemployed.

The Brewery that owns this place supports
only the unambiguously 'male'
Northern working class spectator sports
that suit the image of its butch *Brown Ale*,
that puts hair on your chest, and makes you fight,
and when you're legless makes a man of you!

The *Brown Ale* drinkers watch me as I write:

one front door orange in a row all blue!

Lines to my Grandfathers

I

Ploughed parallel as print the stony earth.
The straight stone walls defy the steep grey slopes.
The place's rightness for my mother's birth
exceeds the pilgrim grandson's wildest hopes—

Wilkinson farmed Thrang Crag, Martindale.

Horner was the Haworth signalman.

Harrison kept a pub with home-brewed ale:

Fell farmer, railwayman, and *publican*,

and he, while granma slaved to tend the vat
graced the rival bars 'to make comparisons',
Queen's Arms, the Duke of this, the Duke of that,
while his was known as just 'The Harrison's'.

He carried cane and *guineas*, no coin baser!
He dressed the gentleman beyond his place
and paid in gold for beer and whisky chaser
but took his knuckleduster, 'just in case.'

II

The one who lived with us was grampa Horner
who, I remember, when a sewer rat
got driven into our dark cellar corner
booted it to pulp and squashed it flat.

He cobbled all our boots. I've got his last.
We use it as a doorstop on warm days.
My present is propped open by their past
and looks out over straight and narrow ways:

the way one ploughed his land, one squashed a rat,
kept railtracks clear, or, dressed up to the nines,
with waxed moustache, gold chain, his cane, his hat,
drunk as a lord could foot it on straight lines.

Fell farmer, railwayman and publican,
I strive to keep my lines direct and straight,
and try to make connections where I can—

the knuckleduster's now my paperweight!

The Earthen Lot

for Alistair Elliot

'From Ispahan to Northumberland, there is no building that does not show the influence of that oppressed and neglected herd of men.'
William Morris, *The Art of the People*

Sand, caravans, and teetering sea-edge graves.

The seaward side's for those of lowly status.
Not only gales gnaw at their names, the waves
jostle the skulls and bones from their quietus.

The Church is a solid bulwark for their betters
against the scouring sea-salt that erodes
these chiselled sandstone formal Roman letters
to flowing calligraphic Persian odes,
singing of sherbert, sex in Samarkand,
with Hafiz at the hammams and harems,
O anywhere but bleak Northumberland
with responsibilities for others' dreams!

Not for the Northern bard the tamarinds
where wine is always cool, and *kusi* hot—

his line from Omar scrivened by this wind 's:

Some could articulate, while others not.

(Newbiggin-by-the-Sea 1977)

Dichtung und Wahrheit

for Marcelino Dos Santos (Frelimo)
Dar-es-Salaam 1971

FRELIMO's fluent propagandist speaks
the cloven tongues of four colonial powers:
French and Spanish, Portugese and ours,
plus Makonde *one* of Mozambique's,
and swears in each the war will soon be won.
He speaks of 'pen & sword', quotes Mao's phrase
about 'all power' the moment his guests gaze
on the 14–18 bronze with Maxim gun.

Dulciloquist Dos Santos, swear to them
whose languages you'll never learn to speak
that tongues of fire at a 1000 rpm
is not the final eloquence you seek.

Spondaic or dactylic those machines
and their dry scansions mean that truths get lost,

and a *pravda* empty as its magazines
is Kalashnikov PK 's flash Pentecost.

Art & Extinction

'When I hear of the destruction of a species I feel as if all the works of some great writer had perished.'
Theodore Roosevelt 1899

I

The Birds of America: John James Audubon (1785–1851)

The struggle to preserve once spoken words
from already too well-stuffed taxonomies
is a bit like Audubon's when painting birds,
whose method an admirer said was this:
Kill 'em, wire 'em, paint 'em, kill a fresh 'un!

The plumage even of the brightest faded.
The artist had to shoot in quick succession
till all the feathers were correctly shaded.

Birds don't pose for pictures when alive!
Audubon's idea of restraint,
doing the Pelican, was 25
dead specimens a day for *one* in paint.

By using them do we save words or not?

As much as Audubon's art could save a,
say, godwit, or a grackle, which he shot
and then saw 'multiplied by Havell's graver'.

II

Standards

in hopeful anticipation of
the bicentenary of the national emblem of
the United States of America
Haliaaetus Falco Leucocephalus, 1782–1982

'Our standard with the eagle stands for us.
It waves in the breeze in almost every clime.'

(The flag, not *Falco Leucocephalus*
poised in its dying on the brink of time!)

Rejecting Franklin's turkey for a bird that *flies*
Congress chose the soaring eagle, called,
for its conspicuous white head, 'the bald'.

Now the turkey's thriving and the eagle dies!

When the last stinks in its eyrie, or falls slow,
when the very last bald eagle goes the way
of all the unique fauna, it won't know
the Earth it plummets to 's the USA.

But will still wing over nations as the ghost
on money, and the mountainous US Post,

much as sunlight shining through the British pound
showed PEACE with her laurels, white on a green ground.

III

Loving Memory

for
Teresa Stratas

The fosses where Caractacus fought Rome
blend with grey bracken and become a blur
above the Swedish Nightingale's last home.

Somehow my need for you makes me seek her.

The Malverns darken as the dusk soaks in.
The rowan berries' dark red glaze grows dull.
The harvest moon's scraped silver and bruised tin
is only one night off from being full.

Death keeps all hours, but graveyards close at nights.
I hurry past the Malvern Hospital
where a nurse goes round small wards and puts on lights
and someone there 's last night begins to fall.

'The oldest rocks this earth can boast', these hills,
packed with extinction, make me burn for you.

I ask two women leaving with dead daffodils:
Where's Jenny Lind's grave, please? They both say: *Who?*

IV

Looking Up

for Philip, Terry, and Will Sharpe
and the bicentenary of the birth of
Peter Mark Roget (1779–1869)

All day till it grows dark I sit and stare
over Herefordshire hills and into Wales.
Reflections of red coals thrown on the air
blossom to brightness as the daylight fails.

An uncharred cherry flaunts a May of flames.
Like chaffinches and robins tongues of fire
flit with the burden of Creation's names
but find no new apostles to inspire.

Bar a farmhouse TV aerial or two,
the odd red bus, the red Post Office van,
this must have been exactly Roget's view,
good Dr. Roget, the *Thesaurus* man.

Roget died here, but 90 when he died
of natural causes, twice as old as me.

Of his six synonyms for suicide
I set myself alight with safe suttee.

V

Killing Time

Among death-protected creatures in a case,
"The Earth's Endangered Species" on display
at a jam-packed terminal at JFK,
killing time again, I see my face
with Hawksbill Turtle, scrimshawed spermwhale bone,
the Margay of the family *Felidae*,
that, being threatened, cost the earth to buy.

And now with scientists about to clone
the long-haired mammoth back from Soviet frost,
my reflection's on the species the World's lost,
or will be losing in a little while,
which, as they near extinction, grow in worth,
the leopard, here a bag and matching purse,
the dancing shoes that were Nile crocodile,

the last *Felis Pardalis* left on Earth,

the poet preserved beneath deep permaverse.

VI

t'Ark

Silence and poetry have their own reserves.
The numbered creatures flourish less and less.
A language near extinction best preserves
the deepest grammar of our nothingness.

Not only dodo, oryx and great auk
waddled on their tod to t'monster ark,
but 'leg', 'night', 'origin' in crushed people's talk,
tongues of fire last witnessed mouthing: *dark*!

Now when the future couldn't be much darker,
there being fewer epithets for sun,
and Cornish and the Togoland *restsprache*
name both the animals and hunter's gun,
celebrate before things go too far
Papua's last reported manucode,
the pygmy hippo of the Cote d'Ivoire,
and Upper Guinea's oviparous toad—

(or mourn in Latin their imminent death,
then translate these poems into *cynghanedd*.)

Acknowledgements

Some of these poems first appeared in *Iron*; *The Listener*; *Planet*; *PN Review*; *Stand*; *Times Literary Supplement*.

First published in the United Kingdom by
Rex Collings Ltd
6 Paddington Street, London W1

ISBN 086036 159 4

Typeset and printed in Great Britain by
Malvern Printers Ltd, Malvern